Unless Restorative Justice

A Case Study from Romania

by Mihail Brînzea, M. Th.

in cooperation with case expert
Daniela V. Ștefănescu

Mihail Brînzea & Daniela V. Ștefănescu

ISBN-13: 978-1546558804

ISBN-10: 1546558802

DEDICATION

To our associates in the Mediator's College - Romania

&

To all seeking real reforms
in the Justice System of the Global Village

CONTENTS

ACKNOWLEDGMENTS

"For as man is the best of the beings when perfected, so he is the worst of all when sundered from law and justice. For unrighteousness is most pernicious when possessed of weapons, and man is born possessing weapons for the use of wisdom and virtue, which it is possible to employ entirely for the opposite ends. Hence when devoid of virtue man is the most unholy and savage of beings, and the worst in regard to sexual indulgence and gluttony. Justice, on the other hand, is an element of the state; for judicial procedure, which means the decision of what is just, is the regulation of the political partnership."

Aristotle, Politics Book 1.1253a1

1

http://www.perseus.tufts.edu/hopper/text?doc=Perseus%3Atext%3A1999.01.0058%3Abo
ok%3D1%3Asection%3D1253a

PREAMBLE

One of the greatest achievements of Restorative Justice Procedures is the fact that the victim can confront the offender in a different environment, in a complete different and safe context, although hurt, more empowered compared at the time when the offence happened.

In countries not legally recognizing the Restorative Practices, the offender is taken by authorities, by the system, hidden from the victim through incarceration, protected - from victims' anger and from social revenge - to be held at least morally accountable for its own very deeds.

In countries not legally recognizing Victim – Offender Conferencing, the offender is simply confronted with the legal terms and statements, laws, by acts of prosecutor and barristers. This type of isolation and confrontation may lead to a behavior based upon the need of the offender to escape from punishment or to defray as less as possible. It furthermore, may lead to a mentality neighboring revenge, as the sentence "we gonna see after I get out" is very well known all over the world.

Keeping apart the victim and the offender, never gives the chance, neither to the offender to start an awareness process through a Restorative Analysis[2] right after the act, nor to the victim to understand "why?" and to get to be empowered by requesting his dignity rights, to hear an appeal of forgiveness and to be able to grant forgiveness, of course in the limits of the legal framework, if any!

Usually, keeping the victim and the offender apart generated even more frustration for the victim, also more ways for the offender to invent for himself the role as a victim and imagine himself as being a "victim of the context." Not to mention the cases when the offender is benefiting of a well-organized and excellent defense, yet the prosecutor is deficient in stating his position … than, at the end of the trial, the offender gets acquittal by the judge and exults over

2 For English speaking readers see Belinda Hopkins, Just Care, Restorative Justice Approaches to Working with Children in Public Care, Jessica Kingsley Publishers, London and Philadelphia, 2009 page 83 sq; For Romanian speaking readers see more on Mihail Brînzea & Ema - Elza Şeclăman, Ghid practic de aplicare a medierii şi practicilor restaurative în mediul educaţional, Fundaţia Centrul de Resurse Juridice – 2012, page 33 sq.

the victim. Then, the victim is deepening its suffering and weakness, but the evildoer gets encouraged. In such a case, the consciousness of both becomes distorted in relation to the real social and justice values, and the confidence of both (victim and offender) regarding the system is flawed in dissimilar ways.

A recent, as 2015, case has shaken Romania, not only through the violence that occurred, but mostly through the reactions and the approaches of the state institutions. The case also shocked through the indeed unexpected public reactions, and the strange opinion of the rural community in which the event occurred. It was extremely surprising how poorly and improperly bodies of justice, media and civil society acted.

FACTS

In short, let us get in the case:

When: 2014, November 10th

What: An 18 year teenage female, student, was raped.

Who offended?: Seven male, between the age of 18 and 27.

Where: Romania, Vaslui County, Valeni village.

A favour for captatio benevolentiae

Monday evening, after classes, a teenage woman, student, was waiting in the bus station intending to go home. An acquainted of her, driving his car, male, 20 years of age, stopped in front of the bus station and asked her if she wants to go home by car, to get home faster. She accepted without questioning his seriousness, especially since he was known to her on a friendly basis.

Thus, a process a captatio benevolentiae, in fact, become a trap, and if we ask ourselves what a process of Restorative Justice could bring to "victim – offender" conferencing (VOC) the first thing we have to state is: THE TRUTH!

As Lorraine Stutzman said: "truth is more than discovery of facts"[3] **It is the time to acknowledge that classic justice is based on facts and findings, which may avoid the truth and the whole truth, sometimes even twist the truth.** However, to the victim, as she knows better than anyone the facts, the truth is the most important. That is why, one of the greatest values of the Victim – Offender Conferencing (VOC) is the TRUTH.

We are going to come back to this, as we will see that during the process, the truth about all that happened was twisted around.

That is why in our opinion VOC, if would have been organized in a safe and structured procedure, ought have been able to bring the truth and to clarify all mythologies and scenarios regarding the event.

---

3 Lorraine Stutzman Amstutz, The Little Book of Victim Offender Conferencing, Good Books, PA 17534, page 22, page 36

Organized gang
Before, during and after the rape

Instead of driving her home, the future offender stopped by the house of another male friend, and they took the teenage woman to a field nearby her village. Furthermore, they called three other friends to participate in the rape[4].

At this point, of the narration, we may say that a Restorative Justice procedure meets a specific need, also a value of the VOC: the <u>accountability</u>. We may see that during investigation and during first phase of the trial, none of the offenders took responsibility for the action. All sex offenders declared that "she wanted it." Furthermore, you may see - down in our case study - that the inhabitants from the village said: "she got what she was looking for"!

However, what we will find is that justice did not prevail and more harm took place that otherwise did not have to take place. If only a Restorative Justice procedure had been followed, things might have turned out differently. Unanswered questions answered.

---

4 http://adevarul.ro/locale/vaslui/video-dezvaluiri-cutremuratoare-cazul-elevei-dinvaslui-violata-sapte-tineri-abuzata-lesin-stropita-alcool-siiarasi-batjocorita-1_5464bba90d133766a8d349f5/index.html

One question unsolved by the ruling from the judge is the answer for the question: Who is responsible? If a VOC would have been organized, the fact that there was a man who refused to participate in the gang rape, surely would have brought more relevance on the question of responsibility. Without VOC, during the first phase of the trial, neither the judge paid any attention to this significant fact, nor the barrister mentioned it. This relevant aspect to the whole process was not even mentioned by authorities, but then, after civic pressure and after a public petition was signed by more than 400.000, the prosecutor took in hearing the man who refused to participate in the rape, and he became a key witness at the end of the process.

Until 22nd of July 2015, media did not know about the 8th man to the group, who refused to rape, and the best testimony for it is the fact that Ion Cristoiu, one of the most notorious and well informed journalists in Romania, mentioned only seven rapists: "In the rape participated in seven guys. Most were called by phone to come and participate. Among these seven guys, none dared to fight the others to save the girl, even to refuse to participate."[5]

Without VOC as legal procedure, the prosecutors and the judges who have been proved as being very mild

5 http://www.nasul.tv/ion-cristoiu-clasa-noastra-politica-a-cazut-la-examenul-violatorii-de-la-vaslui/

to perpetrators (even freed them) have been able to hide the key witness, more than nine months, from November 10th 2014 until August 2015.

If VOC would have taken place, <u>transparency</u>, as a value of VOC would have been provided to the whole process, insuring a "complete and honest understanding of the motivation"[6] of the offenders and of those who abstained.

If VOC would have been a legal and regulated procedure, the **accountability** and the **responsibility** of each in the group would have been structured according to the reality:
- Who planned and made the calls?
- Who from among all that have been called to participate in rape, came?
- Who from among that came, participated in rape?
- Who from among that came DID NOT participate? because "from his point of view, what happened was rape"[7], not sex within the group asked by the victim, as lately the offenders have claimed!!

Those would have been questions helping all parties, but especially the offenders to become aware of what they did, according to their will!

---

6 Lorraine Stutzman Amstutz, The Little Book of Victim Offender Conferencing, Good Books, PA 17534, page 21

7 http://www.nasul.tv/ion-cristoiu-clasa-noastra-politica-a-cazut-la-examenul-violatorii-de-la-vaslui/

The one who refused to participate in the rape made definitely a huge difference, also from a civic and ethical point of view, a difference that could have turned around from the very beginning all the visceral attitude of the community towards the victim, if VOC would have been organized.

Moreover, the attitude of the one who abstained from rape was important, for justice to be done!

Seizure and deprivation of freedom, during the rape and also during investigation

One of the basic and most relevant values of Victim Offender Conferencing is <u>self-determination</u> and "empowerment of all participants".[8]

Doubtless a victim who was seized and deprived of freedom, raped and humiliated in many ways is weakened and needs a real and structured process to be empowered to overcome all the mess she was passing through. Although the empowerment should be for medium and long term, its real start is in the VOC, when the victim confronts the offender in a save environment.

The spoliation of victim's self-determination was a fact nobody can deny! Although the teenager kept

---

8 Lorraine Stutzman Amstutz, Idem, page 22.

crying and imploring the rapist to let her go home, the offender continued to rape and to mock her. Meanwhile, sixth male responded to the rapists' phone calls and arrived to the place. While assaulted, amid the suffering caused, the young woman fainted several times. Nonetheless, the sex offenders had no pity on her. They took from the car a bottle of brandy and sprinkled her face, and then they said: "next in line"[9]. After they raped her, one by one, the six perpetrators boarded into the car and went to another village, called Moara Domneasca (Royal Mill), where they summoned another young man and forced once again the victim to have sexual intercourse, although she could barely stand to her feet, exhausted, yet continued to beseech to leave her alone. After three hours torment, around 22.30, rapists brought the victim at home and asked her not to tell anyone about what happened.

As more offenders came into rape, as lonely and secluded, she felt! Thus, VOC done in a structured way would have regained for the victim the sense of the possibility to confront the offenders, and she would have to feel enabled to confront them.

A VOC process would encourage empowerment of all participants. One who believes that the offenders

---

9 http://adevarul.ro/locale/vaslui/video-dezvaluiri-cutremuratoare-cazul-elevei-dinvaslui-

violata-sapte-tineri-abuzata-lesin-stropita-alcool-siiarasi-batjocorita-

1_5464bba90d133766a8d349f5/index.html

do not need empowerment is delusive, as offenders - according to experts in psychology - oppress others, mostly because they have to balance their weakness, to prove their self-determination, yet having severe cognitive distortions[10]: "offenders often were first victims themselves"[11]Yet, in an attempt to get equilibrium, they do it wrongly! The offender had needed help long before the committal. However, in VOC, offenders have at least the chance to start "Self-Reinforcement" which is the "exercise of self-control used by an individual to reinforce his or her own behavior, by seeing that behavior through the eyes of another"[12]. Here we have a turning point where the victim is actually helping the perpetrator!

Authorities' action and findings

Early evening, the victim's father called the emergency line, announcing his daughter's disappearance. Around 22.30, the girl arrived at home in a wretched state. She recounted what happened to her, and her parents sought assistance from

---

10 Jaydip Sarkar, Mental health assessment of rape offenders,

http://www.ncbi.nlm.nih.gov/pmc/articles/PMC3777344/

11 Lorraine Stutzman Amstutz, Idem, page 64

12 Eric See & Elicia Kieser, Student Study Guide for Criminological Theories: Introduction, Evaluation, Application, Methodist University New York, Sixth Edition By Ronald L. Akers and Christine S. Sellers OXFORD UNIVERSITY PRESS 2013, see Chapter 5 – Social Learning Theory

ambulance, for medical care to be given.[13] The police investigation stated that during the three hours while the teenager was subject to rape, she was called no less than 60 times by parents, friends and colleagues.

"The patient has multiple bruising and was subjected to strong both physical and psychological trauma; she will hardly overcome, requiring psychological counseling and professional help," said Anna Rinder, manager at Vaslui County Emergency Hospital[14]. School Director and the Students' Tutor contacted the victim to provide support. The evaluation stated that the teen must be included within a program of counseling with school psychologists in order to be able to overcome the trauma. Forensic doctors, who examined the young, confirmed that she was the victim of horrific and apallic sexual assaults[15].

Three days after the rape, 13th of November 2014, the seven young men were in kept in detention, according to the ruling of Vaslui Court.[16]

On behalf of Government, the Prime Minister Victor Ponta, himself a former prosecutor, asked Justice

---

13 http://adevarul.ro/locale/vaslui/video-dezvaluiri-cutremuratoare-cazul-elevei-dinvaslui-violata-sapte-tineri-abuzata-lesin-stropita-alcool-siiarasi-batjocorita-1_5464bba90d133766a8d349f5/index.html

14 Ibidem

15 Ibidem

16 http://betaido.infoziare.ro/stire.read.php?newz_id=3821348

Minister to resign if the case is not properly and rightly ruled. Meanwhile the Romanian mass-media, eager for rating, exposed the identity of the victim. The Mass-Media Commission of the Romanian Senate demanded upon the National Audiovisual Council to adopt harsh sanction for the violations regarding the exposure of victims' identity.[17]

The decision to let out the aggressors was contested by politicians, led by Prime Minister Victor Ponta: "I want to express my solidarity not only with the victim, but all victims who have suffered rape and did not yet get justice right. I want to express my outrage that for years we keep saying that justice must punish all perpetrators on equal ground, but especially those who commit murder, rape, robbery".[18]

The comments of Ion Cristoiu, journalist, are highly relevant on the reaction of authorities and political class, regarding the rape: *"I was stunned by the reaction of politicians. Asked about the case, Alina Gorghiu - opposition leader, lawyer and politician who have served as president of the National Liberal Party (PNL) since December 2014; she has been a member of the Romanian Chamber of Deputies, since December 2008 - replied that Victor Ponta [the Prime Minister] must resign! Andreea Vass declared: she does not*

---

17 http://www.reporterntv.ro/stire/marturia-cutremuratoare-a-tinerei-violate-de-sapte-indivizi-imi-este-frica-sa-ies-pe-strada

18 http://stirileprotv.ro/stiri/actualitate/magistratii-care-i-au-lasat-liberi-pe-violatorii-din-vaslui-sunt-cercetati-disciplinar-ce-acuzatii-li-se-aduc.html

deal with rape. She has to handle Rovana Plumb (Since 5th of March 2014, Minister of Labor, Family, Social Protection and Elderly, her political adversary). With few exceptions, among which we include Traian Băsescu (former President of Romania), politicians have refused to express their view, "because it's not their business / job". How come it is not their business? Then which is their job? To topple Victor Ponta (the Prime Minister)? To fight each other? To rob the country? The case from Vaslui County is a case that concerns politicians unavoidably. The case is the radiography of the Romanian society beyond Bucharest nearness, a picture of the muddle and bewilderment of Justice, a picture of the prosecutors' deals and an irrefutable evidence of the indifference proved by the annuitants from the Superior Council of Magistrates"[19].

Indeed, nobody can force a politician to comment, yet if procedures of Restorative Justice would have been legal procedures, the value of <u>interconnectedness</u> would have held also the politicians bound to participate in their capacity as law makers, because Restorative Justice through interconnectedness addresses the "social and systemic implications"[20] of a crime, and turn to a risk assessment and prevention process.

---

19 http://www.nasul.tv/ion-cristoiu-clasa-noastra-politica-a-cazut-la-examenul-violatorii-de-la-vaslui/

20 Lorraine Stutzman Amstutz, Idem, page 21

As you see from above, the carelessness of the political class downcast any chance for a social – systemic approach. To them, the cases become an occasion for political vendetta!

INSTEAD OF TRUE RESTORATIVE JUSTICE

Twisting the basics of Human Rights, Misleading the Act of Justice and the Public

In April 2015, a five months after the rape, the Vaslui Court decided to release the offenders.[21] Please notice that initially, three offenders cooperated with the Prosecutor, recognizing the rape and got an Agreement, being released from custody and placed under judicial control. Later, all seven were placed under the measure of residence arrest and latterly the "measure of residence arrest was replaced by the judiciary control".[22]

When ruling the release from custody of the three who did recognize the crime, Vaslui Court judges

---

21 http://betaido.infoziare.ro/stire.read.php?newz_id=3821348

22 http://betaido.infoziare.ro/stire.read.php?newz_id=3821348

have decided to free the others (four) too, "considering that there should be no discrimination between defendants, having seen that none is known with criminal records, and all had a flawless civic conduct until the rape".[23]

After the release of the offenders, media reacted and the case was widely publicized through social media, especially Facebook. Some NGOs have addressed to Justice Ministry and to the Presidency of Romania the invitation to engage and initiate internal audits regarding the judges and prosecutors responsible with the case.[24]

It seems that the understanding of judges and prosecutors regarding "discrimination" either is very poor, or is a tool for twisting the justice. In the case of the sex offenders, there was no discrimination at all, as three of them recognized the crime and got the so called "Agreement", but the others negated. The release of the three was based on cooperation agreement.

---

23 http://adevarul.ro/locale/vaslui/gest-incalificabil-unuia-cei-7-violatori-vaslui-judecati-libertate-violat-eleva-lesin-o-dau-masina-voi-1_554b9f5ccfbe376e35f435df/index.html the

24 http://betaido.infoziare.ro/stire.read.php?newz_id=3821348

Justice's upheaval
Or playing with postponements

Of note is the fact that until direct involvement of the Association for Implementation of Democracy, through petition issued and registered in June 2015 at the Superior Council of Magistrates (SCM), direct involvement of Adevarul Journal, that started the advocacy campaign for the victim, nothing would have happened! After it the SCM begun to investigate why offenders were freed.[25] Duly, the General Prosecutor informed the Association for Implementation of Democracy that internal inquiry will take place regarding the observance of the procedures and the ruling according to the law[26].

Reactions of Justice Institutions

At Civil Society protests, the magistrates who ruled the release of offenders become subject to disciplinary investigation. The Judicial Inspection of the Superior Council of Magistrates made public that judges who freed the sex offenders and put them under judiciary control measure, were at their turn placed "under disciplinary investigation being under

---

25 http://www.hotnews.ro/stiri-esential-20311644-deputatul-tudor-ciuhodaru-vreau-

violatorii-fie-tratati-condamnati-fel-criminalii-solicit-sprijin-pentru-eliminarea-violulului-din-

legea-medierii.htm

26Ibidem

suspicion of exercising the office in bad faith and through serious negligence".[27]

After the reaction of the Superior Council of Magistrates, the enthusiasm for justice spread and caught others too! Through an Order by Tiberiu Nitu, the General prosecutor, other rapes cases form all over the country were put under inquiry for the suspicion that either judges, either prosecutors have been lax and mild.[28] The courts performing shilly-shally and prevarication were very well known to the authorities[29] as for example the case form Giurgiu Court, 2013, when a girl of 14 years of age, was raped also by seven sex offenders, who tied and raped her. It was well known to the authorities that the offenders from Giurgiu were released as the second day, and also was known that, after two years and a half, the seven perpetrators have not been prosecuted and brought to trial![30] So, those of justice grabbed worthiness! Same happened with the Military Prosecutors who restarted work on rape cases they had postponed for years. [31]

---

27 http://betaido.infoziare.ro/stire.read.php?newz_id=3821348

28 http://adevarul.ro/news/eveniment/victima-lavaslui-violata-doua-oara-comunitate-cad-primele-capete-urmaanchetei-care-i-vizeaza-magistrati-

1_55b50d00f5eaafab2cf56cd4/index.html

29 Ibidem

30 Ibidem

31 Ibidem

Adevarul Journal reported that the General Prosecutor Office started to review all rape cases in which perpetrators were investigated or prosecuted in freedom.[32]

Police Reaction

Meanwhile, as the inhabitants from the Valeni village turned much in the favor of the sex offenders, and the young lady and her family were put under social and psychological pressure; as the supporters of the seven offenders threatened the journalists that they would be raped, and same supporters behaved aggressive, especially in relation to women journalists, the headship of the Police Inspectorate of Vaslui supplemented the number of police to the village".[33]

All the above facts and findings are nothing but proof of an unsafe society, especially for women, and a discovery that the triggers' insecurity had been hidden by the authorities, so that citizens would not have a clue to the magnitude of the occurrence.

If Restorative Justice would have been in place, and Victim - Offender - Community Conferencing would have been properly conducted in the majority of the 6 per day rape cases (reported) that occurred in the last

---

32 Ibidem

33 http://betaido.infoziare.ro/stire.read.php?newz_id=3821348

five years (as police records and statistics state)[34], the phenomenon could tend to alleviation. Fear in the community does not tend to decrease if cases are hidden, but "a community level of fear towards crime tends to decrease when they are part of creating a safer environment and helping to reduce various types of crime"[35]

---

34 http://urbology.ro/totusi-in-romania-au-loc-6-violuri-in-fiecare-zi/

35 Lorraine Stutzman Amstutz, Idem, page 71

STIGMA, DEMONIZATION AND POWER ROLLOVER

Perception and risks

Europe FM correspondent, Sorin Saizu, affirmed that, according to locals, the intense media coverage of the case may influence justice and can be a threat to the fair accomplishment of justice.[36]

However, for the victim, to socialize become the greater risk: I am afraid to walk down the street. They all shout that I am guilty![37]

Ionut Brătianu, psychologist, expressed the risk of suicidal thoughts: The victim's subjective belief can develop some justification: "Why stay alive when nobody understands me, nobody believes me, and I

---

36 http://betaido.infoziare.ro/stire.read.php?newz_id=3821348

37 http://stirileprotv.ro/stiri/actualitate/imi-este-frica-sa-ies-pe-strada-toti-spuneau-ca-eu-sunt-de-vina-eleva-violata-in-vaslui-si-a-povestit-drama-la-maruta.html

belong to nobody, etc. This girl is raped even currently by the community and by the perverse procedures that allow the aggressors to wage a social and moral smear campaign on the victim. It requires medium-term psychological support for both, the victim and the family".[38]

Another risk was identified by psychologist Diana Ioaneş who did psychotherapy with teenagers who endures the trauma of rape. One risk is that parents do not believe the young girl and incline to assign her also a share of blame, and in this case "basically, the victim is raped twice. I have every respect for the girl's parents who have not succumbed to the pressure. The second risk is related to the effects of the abuse: the victim hardly will have a normal relationship with a man, because she will have the feeling of fear, even forever".[39]

An even more specific set of risks were identified by Dan Popescu, a psychotherapist with expertise in counseling abused women and vulnerable groups. He said that the campaign supporting rapists may invalidate the victim as a person. His opinion leads to

---

38 http://adevarul.ro/news/eveniment/victima-lavaslui-violata-doua-oara-comunitate-cad-primele-capete-urmaanchetei-care-i-vizeaza-magistrati-1_55b50d00f5eaafab2cf56cd4/index.html

39 http://adevarul.ro/news/eveniment/victima-lavaslui-violata-doua-oara-comunitate-cad-primele-capete-urmaanchetei-care-i-vizeaza-magistrati-1_55b50d00f5eaafab2cf56cd4/index.html

the idea that the victim would be better off if would move from the county: "When you're the abused, and everyone accuses you of instigation to rape you feel like a stray dog, dehumanized. Psychotherapist Dan Popescu described the victim as trampled upon and destabilized. Her femininity will be much affected. His advice regarding the solution to all these risks would be for the victim to move out of the community, take her family and change the identity, as it is done in the United States in the framework of the program for witness protection. So they will be able to strive for a normal life".[40] In debating some critical aspects regarding this case study, a friend of mine, having a substantial work experience (in Canada) with women in conflict with the law, who was program manager working alongside the women, creating their plans for their reintegration back to the community, Caroline Vuyadinov (Lynch) openly asked: "Why should she have to leave? She did nothing wrong. Why does she have to uproot her life?" I have no proper answer except to tell that in spite of Victim – Offender – Community Conferencing even professionals in Psychotherapy like Dan Popescu cannot think about reintegration of the victim back to normal life within the community. Only in a VOCC things can become cristal-clear and the victim can overcome any suspicion, stigma and blame! According to previous shared experiences,

---

40 Ibidem

merely in a procedural context as VOCC - where victims are empowered to confront in a safe environment, the offenders and the initiators of the slut-shaming campaign – a woman can stop the recurring of rape and rebuild the premises for continuing her life within that community.

Threats, public mocking, slut shaming campaign

As we can establish, stigma was already in place, as the inhabitants from the village say: "She was not good vine! (Romanian expression about women with no moral values) Probably she wants money. I do not know![41]

"She was not an innocent girl" or "she was not the church's door" (i.e pure, chaste)! "These guys have nothing to be blamed for, ... a mistake of their youth. Let me tell you how many she laid with! She got what she was seeking for!", declared few men from the village to journalists.[42]

Psychologist Mihai Copăceanu underlines that "the thought she could have avoided the whole tragedy is another heavy going! Romania has a national problem

---

41 http://stirileprotv.ro/stiri/actualitate/magistratii-care-i-au-lasat-liberi-pe-violatorii-din-vaslui-sunt-cercetati-disciplinar-ce-acuzatii-li-se-aduc.html

42 http://adevarul.ro/news/eveniment/victima-lavaslui-violata-doua-oara-comunitate-cad-primele-capete-urmaanchetei-care-i-vizeaza-magistrati-1_55b50d00f5eaafab2cf56cd4/index.html

on abuses against women, and here I refer to rape, sexual assault, physical violence, trafficking and prostitution. And they all range from failure to respect dignity and rights of women, and from the fact that the social norm perpetuates that man is superior to a woman, and he has the power to do what he wants. And we have a number of myths that reinforce it" said Copăceanu.[43]

One fact should be said firmly: the sex offenders did mock the victim by sprinkling her with alcohol when she was fainting[44], and they did mock her also through social media communications! Friends and family of perpetrators said that "she destroyed seven families" and she was instigating to be raped. The mother of the offender - who accosted the victim in the street under the pretext that he can give her a drive home - started the denigration campaign.[45]

Psychologists say that the public disdain can lead the victim to depression with possible psycho-behavioral non-conformities up to suicide. It was acknowledged

---

43 Ibidem

44 http://adevarul.ro/locale/vaslui/video-dezvaluiri-cutremuratoare-cazul-elevei-dinvaslui-violata-sapte-tineri-abuzata-lesin-stropita-alcool-siiarasi-batjocorita-1_5464bba90d133766a8d349f5/index.html

45 http://adevarul.ro/locale/vaslui/tupeu-mizerabil-celor-sapte-bestii-violat-lesin-eleva-vaslui-nu-fost-viol-ci-sex-surpriza-nu-meritam-5-ani-5-minute-1_55a370f8f5eaafab2c856d7c/index.html

that community support for the rapists is equivalent to a recurring rape.[46]

It is well known that right after the arrest of offenders, their families asked for mercy and offered various amounts of money as compensation for withdrawal of the complaint. Facing refusal, relatives and friends of offenders had accused the victim that she intended a scenario that would have meant to bring her a large sum of money after "staged" gang rape. [47] On the Internet, they launched rumors that she had performed "surprise and group sex".[48]

All the above facts lead to the idea that, beyond Victim – Offender Conferencing, in the village where the rape took place, there was much need to start a management of change, especially Mentality Change process, and the best to begin with, would have been a Community Conference[49], a very powerful procedure in Restorative Justice that contributes much to avoiding the stigma for both, victim and offender. For the community - in order to have a

---

46 http://adevarul.ro/news/eveniment/victima-lavaslui-violata-doua-oara-comunitate-cad-

primele-capete-urmaanchetei-care-i-vizeaza-magistrati-

1_55b50d00f5eaafab2cf56cd4/index.html

47 Ibidem

48 Ibidem

49 Mihail Brînzea & Ema - Elza Șeclăman, Ghid practic de aplicare a medierii și practicilor restaurative în mediul educațional, Fundația Centrul de Resurse Juridice – 2012, page 33 sq.

clear image of what happened – a restorative framing would have been necessary.⌐

Nevertheless, although in Romania there are more than 100 associations dealing with Human Rights, conflict transformation, peace building, community renewal / transformation, victims' assistance, violence against women, etc., up to now none of them made an intervention in the sense of Restorative Justice. A lot of visceral behavior and jeering language would have been avoided if Victim – Offenders – Community Conferencing would have been taken place!

THE NEED FOR PUBLIC ETHICS

Adevarul Journal took the initiative to lead a public campaign for awareness and support for the victim. They asked experts on the phenomenon, and experts unanimously said: "Such acts must be condemned by the community!"[50]

Psychologist Aurora Liiceanu explained that for victims of rape, the only way to continue is accepting the painful past, refusing to make suffering an aim in itself, and activate the desire not to remain anchored in that unhappy time. All victims have a constant struggle for normality.[51]

---

50 http://adevarul.ro/news/eveniment/institutiile-statului-medicul-preotul-trebuie-condamne-violul-1_55b27c58f5eaafab2ce796ee/index.html

51 Ibidem

"The community must condemn and, strongly refute and declare that rape is not acceptable, which means a constant and sustained effort that should be done by the community and local state institutions, regional NGOs, including the doctor and the priest", said psychotherapist Mihai Copăceanu. The same logic and expectations were expressed by sociologist Ciprian Necula, who commented for the National Journal: I saw no message on behalf of the Church or from the priest in that village![52]

Unfair fight for the victim's identity, none but for rating

It is to say that as eager and greedy the media can be for rating, the X TV station succeeded to have the victim's full face broadcasted live. The video recording is even now posted on the Internet. Why? Simply, in Romania, there is no protection for victims of rape identity. That is why 90% of women prefer to remain silent about it.

Anyway, the National Audiovisual Council (NAC) debated about the case and the victim shown by some TV channels. The members of NAC discussed the decision of the TV to reveal the victim's identity. Moreover, Valentin Jucan, member of NAC, stated as

---

52 http://www.realitatea.net/bilan-cutremurator-al-dosarelor-penale-pentru-viol-in-medie-anul-trecut-sase-violuri-pe-zi_1769476.html#ixzz3kDgmSmzl

inadmissible the attitude of the TV station, believing that "X TV Chanel destroyed the teenager's future".[53]

Although the agreement between the victim and the journalist was regarding an interview with a covered face, and the lawyer of the family stated this firmly, the TV team did not keep the word.[54] The mother of the victim stressed that agreements with the television to appear live were signed at the end of the broadcast. "The contracts were signed at the end. They did not tell me that we would sign a contract"[55]

On the other hand, the TV officials argued that both, mother and daughter have signed "personal and voluntary" agreements to participate in the interview, stressing that the TV team explained, "clear and open", how the interview will be conducted.[56]

As for the identity issue: no legislation, no ethical conduct!

Thus, the authorities have seriously to reflect and take action regarding the media – victim relationships in the sense that the victim has to be protected in any manner, and the misuse of victims for rating shall be sanctioned. We do need freedom of media, but not at

---

53 Ibidem

54 Ibidem

55 Ibidem

56 Ibidem

the expense of trampling the intimacy and the identity with the victims of tragic and atrociously events.

Attempt to buy the victim through a notary mediator

Since 2006, Mediation became a legal procedure and a legally regulated profession in Romania through issuing Law 192. The Law 192/2006 was completed and amended a few times and in 2014 it stated that penal mediation may apply to offenses for which, by law, the withdrawal of prior complaint or reconciliation among the parties removes criminal liability, [Art. 67 (1) Law 192/2006] meanwhile Art. 67 (2) is stating that "No victim or the perpetrator may be compelled to accept mediation procedure".

Being advised on the Provisions Of The Law 192/2006, the parents of the perpetrators waited for the young girl to get out from classes and took her to a Public Notary, trying to persuade her to have a Mediation Agreement, to drop the complaint and consequently, to stop the penal action.

Yet, the Public Notary refused the mediation attempts on the ground that the victim come without being accompanied by her parents or by her lawyer[57].

---

57 http://www.agerpres.ro/justitie/2015/07/29/vaslui-fata-violata-de-tinerii-din-valeni-a-fost-dusa-pentru-a-semna-un-acord-de-mediere-notar-19-47-29

Indeed, the Public Notary conducted the tenacious request for Mediation in a very professional way as Art. 68, Law 192/2006 states "(1) mediation in criminal cases must be conducted so that each party is guaranteed the right to legal assistance and if necessary, an interpreter. Minutes taken under this law, which closes the mediation procedure, should show whether the parties have benefited from the assistance from a lawyer and an interpreter or if appropriate, mention that they have expressly waived."

Instead of proper appeal to Mediation, in this case we have non-compliance with legal provisions and procedures, a misuse of potential Alternative Dispute Resolution, an attempt of abusing the law, mostly an attempt to bribe the victim and to enmesh the law.

What if Restorative Justice would have been in place as legal procedure, or at least information concerning VOC and Mediation?

Beginning 1st of August 2013, it was compulsory to attend an information session regarding Mediation[58], just to enable the citizens to take an informed decision and opt, either for Justice in Court or for Mediation. However, since 8th of May 2014 by Decision 266/2014 the Constitutional Court strangely declared Art. 2 (1) from Law 115/2012

---

58 Law 115/2012, Art. 2 (1)

unconstitutional[59]. A very beneficial measure was lost! Instead of seeing as a measure for optimizing the informed choice to access the rights to justice, the Constitutional Court of Romania interpreted it as restricting access to justice. And that is a pity, because in many cases, citizens are not informed about the right to Mediation as a legal procedure, are not informed about the principles and the benefits of it. Moreover, there are attempts to sly and abuse the procedure, as happened in this case.

---

59 Monitorul Oficial, Partea I, nr. 464, 25.06.2014

HATE SPEECH AND THREATS

The Civil Society and the Citizens

An Englishman, Director at Women's Aid Association stated firmly that in England "the perpetrators would have been arrested and would remain in custody.[60] What the director forgot, or the journalist did not record, is the fact that in Great Britain, the Restorative Justice is practiced often, and although perpetrators are held in custody, Restorative Justice would have been part of the legal procedures, since 2012, according to the Justice Minister, Lord McNally, who told The Guardian: "It's been a key policy of the Liberal Democrats for a number of years. We pressed very hard to get a slot for Restorative Justice [in the bill]. We will now put

---

60 http://stirileprotv.ro/stiri/actualitate/magistratii-care-i-au-lasat-liberi-pe-violatorii-din-vaslui-sunt-cercetati-disciplinar-ce-acuzatii-li-se-aduc.html

Restorative Justice on a statutory footing which gives it greater credibility and shows that it is not just a sideshow. It ticks boxes both for those who want to see a more central role for the victim and those who see it as a real factor in rehabilitation."[61]

According to the Ministry of Justice (in Great Britain), surveys on Restorative Justice have found that victims report an 85% satisfaction rate. A drop of around 14% in reoffending rates was recorded among perpetrators.[62] To follow the example of Great Britain would be a milestone for beginning the implementation of a justice reform in Romania.

Later, 15 NGOs made a public call for the Ministry of Justice in Romania for transposing Directive 2012/29/EU on establishing minimum standards on the rights, support, and protection of victims of crime. The network "Break the Silence About Sexual Violence", said they want to know how the rights under the directive of the European Union, psychological counseling and professional assistance, would be regulated in order for the victims to get free legal aid, and granting financial compensation measures to avoid re-victimization.[63]

---

61 Owen Bowcott, More offenders to meet their victims under plan to expand restorative justice, http://www.theguardian.com/uk/2012/oct/30/offenders-meet-victims-plan

62 http://www.theguardian.com/uk/2012/oct/30/offenders-meet-victims-plan

63 http://adevarul.ro/locale/vaslui/scrisoare-deschisa-adresata-ong-uri-presedintelui-

The trial in liberty of the seven sex offenders and the lack of services for victims of sexual assault, did nothing but confirmed once again that preventing and combating violence against women is not a priority for the authorities" said the representative of the Network[64]

As on behalf of the citizens, the petition (to consider rapists as public threat and arrest them) was signed by 402.520 people.[65] Even so, up to this moment, there is no parliamentary initiative to change the law regarding sexual assaults.

Let us see few messages from the public to understand that the laxity and the corruption of authorities may lead to improper approaches, to public anger and to hate speech:

"These guys deserve not only to be imprisoned, tortured, worth tearing their skin, but maybe in jail, they will be "girls" for other convicts, and then they will see how well it is to be raped! If the law does not do its job, then why do we claim to be European country? Those are brutes that deserve maximum

---

iohannis-ministrului-justitiei-cazul-eliberarii-celor-7-tineri-violat-eleva-vaslui-

1_558c462ccfbe376e359ba4a0/index.html

64 http://adevarul.ro/locale/vaslui/scrisoare-deschisa-adresata-ong-uri-presedintelui-

iohannis-ministrului-justitiei-cazul-eliberarii-celor-7-tineri-violat-eleva-vaslui-

1_558c462ccfbe376e359ba4a0/index.html

65 http://www.petitieonline.com/forum/137279/start/0

punishment! Lack of education leads to something like this, and society is to be blamed ... o, hear; villagers keep their side [perpetrators side] because mommy and daddy have big property and car! Be ashamed dear Romanians! Freedom is a right that you are born with, yet if you do not know to discern, and use it right, it is better to be deprived of liberty if you're a danger for the society. Maximum penalty for the seven defendants!"[66]

"If they would not be arrested, take the mace and run after them!"[67]

"Chemical castration for all seven! Mercilessly! These animals are not worthy of anything"[68]

"I'm a father. And I have a daughter. Hand on heart I say: If this would have happened to my daughter, all seven would not have been alive up to this very moment. I would have devoured all of them in one day! I wouldn't care to go to jail afterwards, but annoyed that I freed the earth of seven jerks."[69]

And we may go on and on, counting more than 400.000 messages of real hate speech and threats, as effect of not having in place at least the VOC as

---

66 Idem, comentariul nr.#8

67 Idem, comentariul nr.#3

68 Idem, Comentariul nr. #9

69 Idem Comentariul #44200

Restorative Justice procedure, but authorities with crafty behavior, who do not give the chance to offenders to say "I am sorry", and to the victim to hear and see the offenders truthfully repenting for what they have done!

The breadth of rape in Romania

"In Romania, in the 21st Century, 2,500 rapes occur annually. One case every four hours! Because such things should not repeat I call for support for a package that provides for the abolition of Mediation procedure in case of rape, and decades of hard jail for sexual abuse. The penalties should be tougher, as the death penalty does not exist in Romania"[70], said Tudor Ciuhodaru, Deputy in the Chamber of Commons.

What a message! Powerful! Tough! Exulting exclusively towards Punitive Justice and attacking any attempt towards Restorative Justice. The politician smelled people's anger and in line with them regrets that the death penalty cannot be sentenced. The empathy of the political man totally joins the ... popular anger! ... or populist? The politician who should propose laws and measures for justice to be done, does not think about the victim at all. In the

---

70 http://www.hotnews.ro/stiri-esential-20311644-deputatul-tudor-ciuhodaru-vreau-violatorii-fie-tratati-condamnati-fel-criminalii-solicit-sprijin-pentru-eliminarea-violulului-din-legea-medierii.htm

above statement, reported by the media, the victim does not even exist. The mind of the political man goes only in the direction of the extreme punishment of perpetrators and proposes harsher punishments.

To the politician, the victim does not exist anymore! She just triggered a media event in which politicians would fish for more votes.

"Break the Silence about Sexual Violence" (a civic networking) and the "Network for Preventing and Combating Violence against Women", draw attention upon the fact that in Romania, there are six sex assaults reported every day, and for sure many others not at all reported, because victims are ashamed and of course afraid, as they are unprotected by the law and authorities. "In 2014, the Romanian Police registered only 875 rapes and the Prosecution has indicted only 469 individuals for this type of crime. Nevertheless, the number of cases of sexual violence is much higher"[71]

Statistics show that 90% of victims know the rapist, nearly 45% of victims are under 25 years of age and unfortunately only 15% of victims are addressing the authorities their case, so they could take action against the perpetrators. The rest, estimated as 85%, do not

---

71 http://www.realitatea.net/bilan-cutremurator-al-dosarelor-penale-pentru-viol-in-medie-anul-trecut-sase-violuri-pe-zi_1769476.html#ixzz3kDgmSmzl

tell anyone about what happened, which amplifies trauma and more.[72]

As regarding the breadth of rape in Romania "the fact that some locals came to the defense of rapists should not be a surprise. They also voted one: Vaslui Deputy, Dan Bordeianu was convicted for rape in 1985.[73]

Mass-Media, via Adevarul Journal, has proven it persuaded in a manner that led authorities to draw from community people who are a public threat, but this does not solve the problem and the possibilities of mass media seem to be limited, as the perpetrators have already made war on journalists. One of the seven offenders threatened journalists attending the trial at Vaslui Court. The perpetrator said that one day he will "run her over a car on the crosswalk".[74] "We gonna gather all from the village and rape you, so you might see what rape means! She is guilty said villagers while threatening the journalists with death."[75]

---

72 http://adevarul.ro/news/eveniment/institutiile-statului-medicul-preotul-trebuie-condamne-violul-1_55b27c58f5eaafab2ce796ee/index.html

73 http://www.realitatea.net/bilan-cutremurator-al-dosarelor-penale-pentru-viol-in-medie-anul-trecut-sase-violuri-pe-zi_1769476.html#ixzz3kDgmSmzl

74 http://adevarul.ro/locale/vaslui/gest-incalificabil-unuia-cei-7-violatori-vaslui-judecati-libertate-violat-eleva-lesin-o-dau-masina-voi-1_554b9f5ccfbe376e35f435df/index.html

75 http://adevarul.ro/locale/vaslui/vom-aduna-satul-vom-viola-vedeti-inseamna-viol-fata-e-vina-satenii-valeni-i-au-amenintat-jurnalisti-moartea-1_55b0eb28f5eaafab2cdc7c33/index.html

No end for the story

The seven offenders were rushed in custody right after the judge sentenced. To the three defendants who admitted the facts, the judge gave incarceration for five years and eight months; the judge sentenced eight years and four months in prison for those who did not plead guilty. A c in amount of 50,000 Lei (about 12.000 Euros) to be paid to the victim was also decided.⌐

Few things are to be considered:

Perpetrators will come from jail most inveterate; their families will embitter as their children amass day after day in a dungeon, and probably the victim and her family will have to move from their village as almost everyone blames the woman!

As for the victim, she would not have the chance to hear why the rape happened?

She can guess, as she told to Larisa Toma, that the offender who took her by car from the bus station, being a former friend of her "wanted more" [i.e. wanted to have sexual relations], but she did not want, she resisted and end the relationship. She has a vague hunch that the rape in the group was a sort of revenge over her refusal.[76] However, she does not know!

Yet, how can she find out without Victim – Offender Conferencing!

---

76 http://stirileprotv.ro/stiri/actualitate/imi-este-frica-sa-ies-pe-strada-toti-spuneau-ca-eu-sunt-de-vina-eleva-violata-in-vaslui-si-a-povestit-drama-la-maruta.html

AFTERWORD

Many friends asked me why do I advocate so much for Restorative Justice, for Victim – Offender Conferencing (VOC), and even for Victim – Offender – Community Conferencing (VOCC). I was also asked why did I choose this case for the current study, and for pleading VOCC.

First, as I said above in this work, the victim and the offender do not need to know more of the reality. They partook in the reality of their case, and they know the facts to a greater degree than any expert who could interrogate them, better than any barrister who would present their case to the court, more than any prosecutor or judge, who will study the proofs and hear the witnesses.

What they both need is the truth about and from behind the facts, and VOCC is the only chance for them to find out. Before the offender goes to prison and gets even more bitter and angry, before the family of the offender threatens the victim every day with death, before the victim gets so scared that her life becomes horrible, so that she has to sell everything and move into another place, the victim and the offender could have the legal chance to hear each other under the guidance of a moderator, in a safe context where the victim would be empowered to hear the truth, and the offender empowered to tell the truth.

I choose this case as I think it is relevant not only for Victim – Offender Conferencing (VOC), but also for Victim – Offender – Community Conferencing (VOCC).

As for the issue of confidentiality, it is to say that by sunrise all inhabitants from Valeni village and from Vaslui town knew about the rape and also the identity of the victim. As much as I know about confidentiality in Restorative Justice procedures, as much I state that, regarding this case, any confidentiality procedure became irrelevant. Confidentiality could only have brought more blame and gossiping about the victim, more public disgrace and abuse, as, in fact, happened.

What could have been better if Victim – Offender – Community Conferencing would have taken place?

Let us see:
1. No one could hide anymore who made the calls to organize the gang rape.

2. No one could hide that there was a man called to participate in the rape who refused to do it. This man, although known to the authorities, became a key witness only after the media campaign made investigations and the Assciation for Implementation of Democracy petitioned the Superior Council of Magistrates, and an internal auditing started.

3. Police, Prosecution Office, Court of Judges, Barristers could not have forgotten about and avoid the key witness during the first stages of the investigation and the trial.

4. The so called "slut-shaming campaign" started by the families of the perpetrators would not have taken place.

5. Instead of more than 400,000 hate messages, a civic, legal approach would have generated more awareness of the horrors of rape, than public expectations that the perpetrators would have to get the same rape treatment in prison.

6. The misuse of the victim's identity for media rating would have had been avoided.

7. Misuse of the Law on Mediation and the twisting by judges on Human Rights and discrimination issues would have had been avoided.

8. The attempts to bribe, directed either to investigators, authorities or to the victim, would have been forgotten from the very beginning, thus VOCC could have also play the role of a powerful tool against corruption.

9. The community, involved anyway by different actors through rumors mocking the victim,

would have been properly involved after ought have understood what really happened.

These are the most significant aspects I wanted to highlight and bring them as support for advocating the legislative initiatives for VOC and when applicable Victim – Offender - Community Conferencing.

I hope this case study will be of benefit to law students, law professors, politicians and all those working in the Civil Society for reforms in Justice.

ABOUT THE AUTHOR

Mihail Brînzea, was born in Comarnic,
Prahova Valey, Romania, in 1962.

He studied Theology and Economics.

For 20 years, he was involved in fundraising and
management for projects related to Human Rights, Anti-
Discrimination, Poverty Alleviation and Combating of
Social Exclusion, Peace Building and Ecumenical Relations
for Development.

In 2010, he was authorized as Mediator according to the
Legal Provisions Of Law 192/2006.

He is a funding member of the College of Mediators,
professional body of mediators in Romania.

Author of:
> *"Practical Guide for Using Mediation and
> Restorative Practices in the Educational System"*
> (2012, in Romanian Language).

Coordinator and Cases Expert on:
> *1. "Guide for Mentality Change Activities in
> Community"* (2009, in Romanian Language)
> *2. "Guide on approaching and solving process
> conflicts"* (2016, in Romanian Language)
> *3. "Guide on approaching and solving
> participation conflicts"* (2016, in Romanian
> Language)

Funding President of the "Infrastructure for Peace
Romania" Networking (I4P – Romania), 2016.

**Currently, Mihail Brinzea is the Executive President of the
"Regional Forum for Human Rights in Romania"**

ABOUT THE CASE EXPERT

Daniela V Ștefanescu

She studied Law.

During the last four years, she was involved in Alternative Dispute Resolution, Human Rights, and Peace Building projects.

In 2012, she was authorized as Mediator according to the Legal Provisions Of Law 192/2006.

She is member in the College of Mediators, professional body of mediators in Romania.

She was Key Expert for:
> 1. *"Guide on approaching and solving process conflicts"* (2016, in Romanian Language)
> 2. *"Guide on approaching and solving participation conflicts"* (2016, in Romanian Language)

Member of the Constitutive Committee of the "Infrastructure for Peace Romania" Networking (I4P – Romania), 2016.

Currently, Daniela V. Ștefănescu is the Vice - President of the "Regional Forum for Human Rights in Romania"